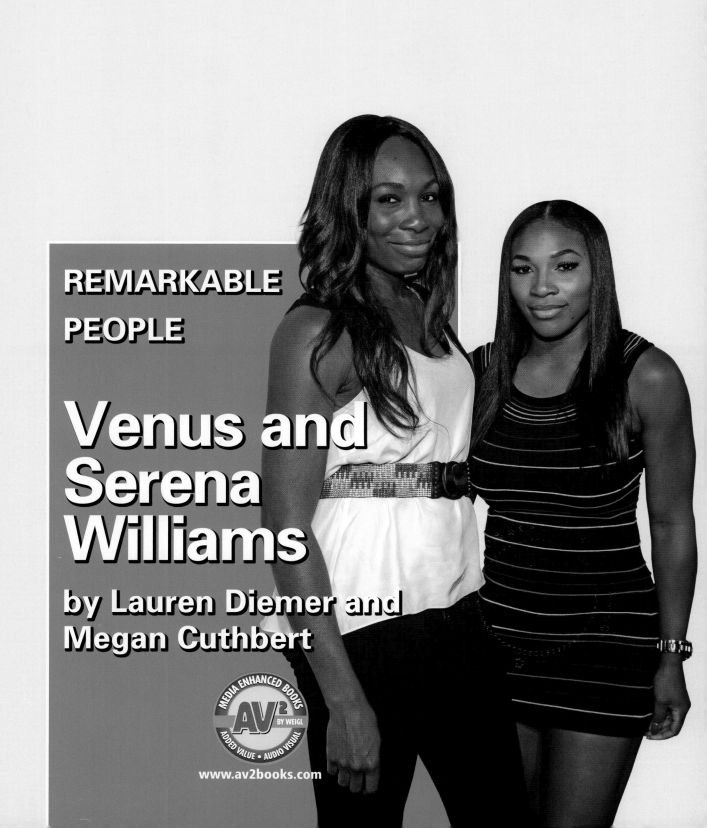

REMARKABLE

PEOPLE

Venus and Serena Williams

by Lauren Diemer and Megan Cuthbert

MEDIA ENHANCED BOOKS

AV2
BY WEIGL

ADDED VALUE • AUDIO VISUAL

www.av2books.com

MEDIA ENHANCED BOOKS
AV²
BY WEIGL™
ADDED VALUE • AUDIO VISUAL

AV² provides enriched content that supplements and complements this book. Weigl's AV² books strive to create inspired learning and engage young minds in a total learning experience.

Your AV² Media Enhanced books come alive with...

Audio
Listen to sections of the book read aloud.

Key Words
Study vocabulary, and complete a matching word activity.

Video
Watch informative video clips.

Quizzes
Test your knowledge.

Embedded Weblinks
Gain additional information for research.

Slide Show
View images and captions, and prepare a presentation.

Try This!
Complete activities and hands-on experiments.

... and much, much more!

Go to **www.av2books.com**, and enter this book's unique code.

BOOK CODE

B 1 7 8 9 1 6

AV² by Weigl brings you media enhanced books that support active learning.

Published by AV² by Weigl
350 5th Avenue, 59th Floor
New York, NY 10118

www.av2books.com   www.weigl.com

Library of Congress Cataloging-in-Publication Data

Diemer, Lauren.
 Venus & Serena Williams / Lauren Diemer and Megan Cuthbert.
     p. cm. -- (Remarkable people)
 Includes index.
 Summary: "Explores the life and times of Venus and Serena Williams, providing an in-depth look at the inspiration, achievements, and successes that define them. Intended for fourth to sixth grade students"--Provided by publisher.
 ISBN 978-1-62127-393-6 (hardcover : alk. paper) -- ISBN 978-1-62127-399-8 (softcover : alk. paper)
 1. Williams, Venus, 1980- 2. Williams, Serena, 1981- 3. African American women tennis players--Biography. 4. Women tennis players--United States--Biography. I. Cuthbert, Megan. II. Title.
 GV994.A1D54 2013
 796.3420922--dc23
 [B]
                        2012041042

Printed in the United States of America in North Mankato, Minnesota
1 2 3 4 5 6 7 8 9 0 17 16 15 14 13

032013
WEP300113

Editor: Heather Kissock
Design: Terry Paulhus

Photograph Credits
Weigl acknowledges Getty Images as the primary image supplier for this title. Every reasonable effort has been made to trace ownership and to obtain permission to reprint copyright material. The publishers would be pleased to have any errors or omissions brought to their attention so that they may be corrected in subsequent printings.

Contents

Who Are Venus and Serena Williams?

Venus and Serena Williams are two of the best female tennis players in the world. They also happen to be sisters. Venus and Serena have each dominated the sport of tennis as **singles** champions. Serena has won 15 **Grand Slam** singles titles, and Venus has won seven. Each woman has been ranked as the number one female tennis player in the world. The two women also combine their skills to play as a **doubles** team. Together, the sisters have won 13 Grand Slam titles as doubles players. Serena has also won two Grand Slams in **mixed** doubles.

"Family's first, and that's what matters most. We realize that our love goes deeper than the tennis game." —Serena Williams

The sisters' hard work and **perseverance** have resulted in success off the court as well. Both Venus and Serena have their own clothing lines. Venus also owns an interior design company, and Serena has been involved in television and film.

Growing Up

Venus Williams was born on June 17, 1980, to Richard and Oracene Williams. Her younger sister, Serena, was born a little over a year later, on September 26, 1981. Venus and Serena were the youngest of five daughters. The three oldest sisters, Yetunde, Lyndrea, and Isha, were Oracene's daughters from her first marriage.

The Williams family moved to Compton, California, shortly after Serena was born. It was a tough neighborhood, where violence and poverty were a part of everyday life. Richard and Oracene wanted to teach their daughters that they could have a better life if they studied and worked hard.

After watching a tennis **match** on television, Richard decided to teach himself how to play the sport. He read books and watched videos to learn the rules and different **techniques**. With Oracene's help, Richard began teaching Venus and Serena how to play. The girls played on the public courts near their home. The courts were not in very good condition, but the girls still practiced daily for two to six hours at a time.

■ When Richard first began teaching Venus and Serena how to play tennis, they used worn rackets and old tennis balls. Despite this, Venus and Serena stayed motivated to improve their tennis abilities.

Get to Know California

FLOWER
California
Poppy

TREE
California
Redwood

BIRD
California Quail

California has a population of more than 37 million people. It has the highest population of any state in the United States.

California has the highest and lowest places in the mainland United States. Mount Whitney is 14,495 feet (4,418 meters) high, and Badwater Basin in Death Valley is 282 feet (85.5 m) below sea level.

The world's largest living tree is in Sequoia National Park in California. The tree's trunk measures 102 feet (31 m) around the base. It also has the largest trunk volume of any tree in the world.

Every year, about 10,000 earthquake tremors occur in southern California.

BADWATER BASIN
282 FEET/855 METERS
BELOW SEA LEVEL

Think about it!

It takes hard work and dedication to become successful. Venus and Serena Williams had to work very hard to achieve their success. Do you think there is anything you could dedicate yourself to like Venus and Serena have? Are you passionate about it? Could you devote your whole life to your passion?

Practice Makes Perfect

Both Venus and Serena began playing in **junior competitions** before the age of five. It was not long before they were at the top of their age divisions. They became well-known throughout the state, and the national media took notice. Several national newspapers interviewed the promising young tennis players.

In 1990, the family moved to Florida so that the girls could attend a well-respected tennis academy. At the academy, the girls practiced six hours each day, six days per week. They spent so much time playing tennis, Richard became worried that his daughters would get tired of the sport. He withdrew them from competitions. Richard wanted his daughters to focus on their education and on practicing their game.

■ Ever since they were children, Venus and Serena have been each other's best friend and toughest rival.

After four years, Richard decided to withdraw both Venus and Serena from the academy. He once again took full responsibility for their tennis coaching. Venus was 14 years old. At that age, **amateur** tennis players could start entering **professional** tournaments.

QUICK FACTS

- By the age of 10, Venus's serve topped 100 miles (161 kilometers) per hour.

- Today, Venus has the fastest woman's tennis serve ever recorded. It was clocked at 129 miles (208 km) per hour.

- The Williams sisters have won a gold medal in the doubles competition at every Olympic games they have entered.

■ Richard Williams had a shopping cart full of tennis balls that he brought with him to the courts every day. He had to remove the middle row of seats in the family's van to get the shopping cart in.

Key Events

On October 31, 1994, Venus became a professional tennis player. At her first professional competition in Oakland, California, the 14-year-old girl managed to hold her own against some of the best female tennis players in the world. The next year, Serena entered her first professional tournament in Quebec, Canada. Unlike her sister, her performance did not make an impact. Richard continued to limit the number of competitions the girls entered. He did not want them to get overwhelmed by the demands of playing tennis professionally. Venus and Serena's skills continued to develop. As they won more matches, their **ranking** in the world continued to climb.

In 1999, Serena was the first Williams sister to win a Grand Slam title. She won the U.S. Open, the lowest **seeded** player ever to do so. Serena was only the second African American woman to win a Grand Slam title. The following year, Venus won the U.S. Open and another Grand Slam title, Wimbledon. In 2002, Venus was officially ranked the number one female tennis player in the world. She was the first African American to reach this position. After five months on top, Venus lost the number one ranking to her sister.

■ Serena had only been competing professionally for two years when she won her first U.S. Open title in 1999.

Thoughts from Venus and Serena

Venus and Serena Williams share their thoughts on winning, losing, and maintaining their relationship.

Serena on playing against her sister.

"We'll battle each other like nobody's business, but the competition will never separate us."

Venus believes she always has a chance to win.

"If the Sun comes up, I have a chance."

Serena believes in finding the positive in all situations.

"The trick...is to find some takeaway moment in the fizzle and carry that with you...aim high...if I fall short of the mark it was still worth doing."

Serena talks about life after tennis.

"I think it's important to just have a normal life because at the end of the day I'm not going to be playing till I'm a hundred."

Venus explains why losing is important.

"When you lose, you're more motivated. When you win, you fail to see your mistakes and probably no one can tell you anything."

Venus talks about her motto.

"My motto has always been that you can't say, 'Oh, it won't happen to me.' You have to say, 'That can happen to me.' So always be aware that things can happen."

What Is a Tennis Player?

Tennis is a sport played between two single players or two teams of two. They face off against each other on either side of a tennis court, separated by a net. Tennis players use racquets to hit a ball over the net to their opponent. Players hit the ball back and forth. The goal is to make the other player miss the ball.

Tennis players must be very fit and strong. They must run back and forth across the tennis court and hit the ball very hard with their racquet. Professional tennis players like Venus and Serena Williams can hit the ball more than 100 miles (161 km) per hour.

Intelligence is very important in tennis. A player must be able to figure out where his or her opponent is going to hit the ball. Then, the player can work out a plan as to how he or she wants to hit the ball back to the other player. **Accuracy** is also important. If a tennis player can hit the ball so that it lands along the **baseline**, it is harder for his or her opponent to return the ball.

■ On July 7, 2012, Venus and Serena won the ladies' doubles title at Wimbledon. Their opponents were Andrea Hlavackova and Lucie Hradecka of the Czech Republic.

Tennis Players 101

Billie Jean King (1943–)

Billie Jean King is one of the best female tennis players of all time. She won 39 Grand Slam titles, including 20 titles at Wimbledon. Her Wimbledon titles record still stands. The U.S. National Tennis Center in New York has been renamed the USTA Billie Jean King National Tennis Center to honor Billie Jean's accomplishments in tennis.

Roger Federer (1981–)

Roger Federer was born in Switzerland in 1981. He is considered to be one of the best tennis players of all time. Roger has won 17 Grand Slam titles and was ranked as the number one male tennis player for a total of 302 weeks. He won the Laureus World Sportsman of the Year award for a record four years in a row, from 2005 to 2008.

Maria Sharapova (1987–)

Maria Sharapova was born in Russia. She is a very successful tennis player. She has won a total of four Grand Slam titles and has been ranked as the number one female player in the world. In 2012, Maria won the silver medal at the London Olympics. Maria's success on the court has led to several endorsement deals.

Steffi Graf (1969–)

Steffi Graf is one of the world's most respected female tennis players. She held the number one ranking for 186 weeks in a row and has won 22 Grand Slam titles. In 1988, she completed the Golden Slam, winning all four Grand Slam tournaments and the Olympic gold medal in the same year. In 1998, Steffi founded Children for Tomorrow, an organization that helps children who have become victims of war and violence.

Endorsements

Although tennis tournaments offer cash prizes for tennis players, many players **supplement** their income with endorsements. Endorsements are deals a company makes to pay a person to promote a product. Often, companies use well-liked and respected athletes, including tennis players, to promote sales of their products.

Influences

Richard and Oracene Williams have had a major impact on their daughters' lives. Neither parent was professionally trained in tennis, but they both helped teach Venus and Serena the game. When the girls were young, Richard's focus was on Venus. She was older and showed more skill than her younger sister. Serena spent most of her time practicing with her mother. Serena's training was more intense and seemed less fun than Venus's training with Richard. Oracene's intensity and no-nonsense demeanor, however, helped Serena's game.

Over the years, Richard and Oracene continued to play an important role in the development of their daughters' talent. However, as the girls became more established in the tennis world, Richard and Oracene's roles decreased. They still support their daughters and are often seen cheering from the stands.

On March 2, 2009, Billie Jean King presented Serena with the top prize when she beat Venus at the BNP Paribas Showdown for the Billie Jean King Cup.

When they were young, Venus and Serena Williams met one of their tennis idols, Billie Jean King. Billie Jean was holding a tennis clinic in a suburb near Compton. Venus and Serena went to the clinic to get training tips from Billie Jean, who was one of the best tennis players in the world.

As well as being a skilled tennis player, Billie Jean also fought for **gender equality** in tennis. One of her biggest struggles was to convince tennis competitions to pay the same amount of prize money to male and female tennis players. This became an important issue for Venus as well. In 2006, Venus wrote an essay in the *London Times* about the issue. It gained worldwide attention. In 2007, Wimbledon agreed to pay equal prize money for the women's tournament. Wimbledon was the last of the Grand Slam tournaments to agree to award equal prize money to women.

THE FAMILY

Richard Williams married Oracene Price in 1980. Oracene was a widow with three young daughters from her first marriage. Richard and Oracene taught the three oldest daughters tennis as well, but they did not have as much talent as their younger sisters. In 2002, Richard and Oracene divorced.

■ The Williams family is very supportive of one another. In 1994, Serena and her parents attended Venus's professional debut at the Bank of the West Classic.

Overcoming Obstacles

It has been difficult for Venus and Serena to juggle being sisters and competitors. They know each other's strengths and weaknesses. This makes them an ideal doubles team. However, when they play against each other in singles matches, they both want to win. In 1998, the girls faced off against each other at the Australian Open. It was the first time they played each other in a Grand Slam title. Venus won the match. The women have since played each other in more than 20 matches, including eight Grand Slam finals. Venus and Serena use the competition to push each other to improve.

Professional athletes must practice constantly. This puts strain on their bodies. Both Venus and Serena have had to deal with injuries at different points in their career. Each time, the Williams sisters have bounced back.

■ It is important for professional athletes to take measures to prevent injuries. At the 2002 U.S. Open, Venus had her hand taped to protect it from a blister.

In 2011, Venus was diagnosed with Sjogren's Syndrome. This disease causes the body's cells to attack the saliva and tear glands. The disease left Venus very tired and sore. She decided she did not want it to rule her life. She changed her diet to help control the **symptoms**.

Serena also faced a health crisis in 2011. Doctors discovered a **blood clot** in her lungs. She needed to take time off from tennis to recover. Many people believed that both women would retire because of their health problems. Neither Venus nor Serena was ready to give up. They attended the 2012 Summer Olympics in London, where Serena won the gold medal in singles tennis. She received another gold medal, along with her sister, when they won the women's doubles competition.

■ On Day 9 of the 2012 Olympics, Serena and Venus were awarded gold medals for their victory in women's doubles tennis. The pair won every set throughout their five matches in London.

Achievements and Successes

Both Venus and Serena have won an impressive number of Grand Slam titles. They have both been ranked as the number one female tennis player in the world more than once. As a doubles team, the Williams sisters have completed a Golden Slam. In 2012, Serena also completed a Golden Slam as a singles player. She is the first player ever to achieve a Golden Slam as both a singles and doubles player.

The Williams sisters are aware that they cannot continue playing professional tennis forever. Both have pursued careers off the court. Venus began studying interior design just as her tennis career was taking off. In 2002, she started V Starr Interiors. Venus then began studying fashion design and started her own line of clothing, EleVen. Like her older sister, Serena also studied fashion design and began a clothing line, Aneres. Serena has also pursued a career in acting. She has appeared in several television shows and movies.

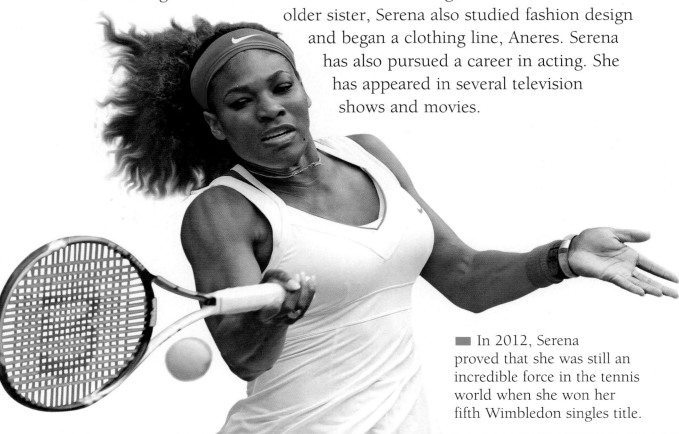

■ In 2012, Serena proved that she was still an incredible force in the tennis world when she won her fifth Wimbledon singles title.

In 2009, Serena and Venus became part-owners of the Miami Dolphins football **franchise**. No other African American women have owned a National Football League team before. Despite their other interests, tennis remains the primary focus for the Williams sisters.

HELPING OTHERS

Venus and Serena Williams have achieved success through hard work and education. These are values they try to encourage through their charitable work. Both sisters are supporters of the Owl Foundation. The foundation was set up by their mother to fund learning programs for students who are struggling in school. Venus and Serena also participate in a number of **exhibition** tennis matches to raise money for charities. In November 2012, they conducted clinics and held exhibition matches in South Africa and Nigeria. The aim of the tour was to promote women's rights. Venus works with UNESCO to promote gender equality throughout the world. She was given the official title of "UNESCO Promoter of Gender Equality." Serena has opened a school in Kenya, the Serena Williams Secondary School.

Write a Biography

A person's life story can be the subject of a book. This kind of book is called a biography. Biographies describe the lives of remarkable people, such as those who have achieved great success or have done important things to help others. These people may be alive today, or they may have lived many years ago. Reading a biography can help you learn more about a remarkable person.

At school, you might be asked to write a biography. First, decide who you want to write about. You can choose a professional tennis player, such as Venus or Serena Williams, or any other person. Then, find out if your library has any books about this person. Learn as much as you can about him or her. Write down the key events in this person's life. What was this person's childhood like? What has he or she accomplished? What are his or her goals? What makes this person special or unusual?

A concept web is a useful research tool. Read the questions in the following concept web. Answer the questions in your notebook. Your answers will help you write a biography.

Venus and Serena Williams

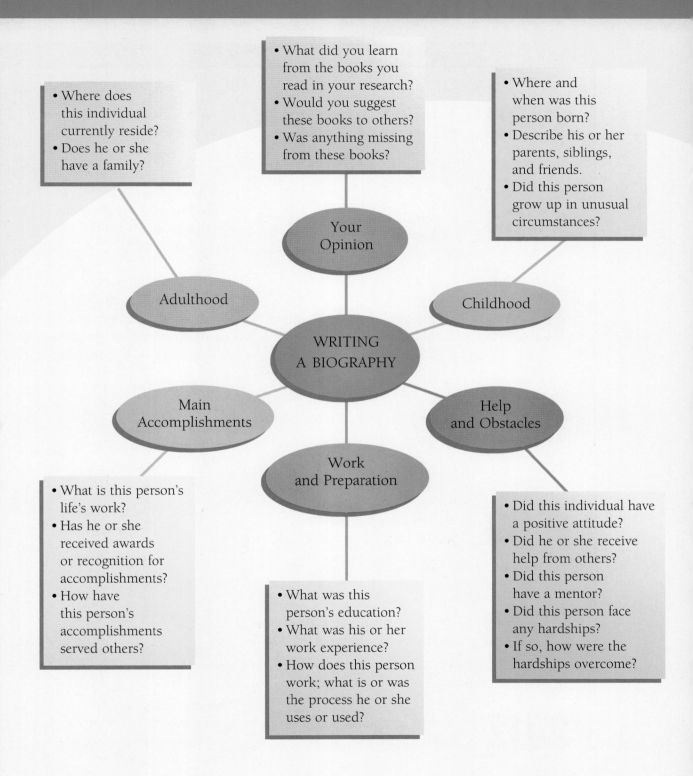

- Where does this individual currently reside?
- Does he or she have a family?

- What did you learn from the books you read in your research?
- Would you suggest these books to others?
- Was anything missing from these books?

- Where and when was this person born?
- Describe his or her parents, siblings, and friends.
- Did this person grow up in unusual circumstances?

Your Opinion

Adulthood

Childhood

WRITING A BIOGRAPHY

Main Accomplishments

Help and Obstacles

Work and Preparation

- What is this person's life's work?
- Has he or she received awards or recognition for accomplishments?
- How have this person's accomplishments served others?

- What was this person's education?
- What was his or her work experience?
- How does this person work; what is or was the process he or she uses or used?

- Did this individual have a positive attitude?
- Did he or she receive help from others?
- Did this person have a mentor?
- Did this person face any hardships?
- If so, how were the hardships overcome?

Timeline

YEAR	VENUS AND SERENA	WORLD EVENTS
1980	Venus is born on June 17, in Lynwood, California.	The U.S. **boycotts** the Summer Olympics in Moscow.
1981	Serena is born on September 26, in Saginaw, Michigan.	Muhammad Ali retires from boxing with a career record of 56 wins and five defeats.
1994	Venus becomes a professional tennis player.	Wayne Gretzky scores his 802nd goal and sets a new record for the most goals scored in a career in the National Hockey League.
1995	Serena becomes a professional tennis player.	National Basketball Association star Michael Jordan announces he is coming out of retirement.
1999	Serena wins the U.S. Open, her first Grand Slam title.	The U.S. Women's soccer team wins the **FIFA** Women's World Cup.
2002	Venus is ranked the number one female tennis player in the world.	The Anaheim Angels win the Major League Baseball World Series for the first time.
2012	Serena completes a singles Golden Slam.	London hosts the Olympic games for the third time. It is the most times any city has hosted the Olympics.

Key Words

accuracy: to be exact and precise

amateur: someone who does not compete for money

baseline: the line that marks the boundaries of a tennis court

blood clot: when blood thickens and blocks a blood vessel

boycotts: to not attend an event as a way of protesting

doubles: tennis match played by two players facing off against two opponents

exhibition: a match played for entertainment, not for competition

FIFA: the international association that governs professional soccer

franchise: the right to own and operate a professional sports team

gender equality: equal rights for men and women

Grand Slam: one of the major four tennis tournaments, which are the Australian Open, U.S. Open, French Open, and Wimbledon. Winning all four major tennis tournaments in the same year is referred to as a Grand Slam

junior competitions: amateur tennis competitions played by young tennis players

match: a contest between players in a sport

mixed: when a team has both male and female players

perseverance: continued effort to reach a goal

professional: playing tennis as a career

ranking: a person's position in a scale of achievement

seeded: the rankings of players in a tournament

singles: tennis match played with one player against a single opponent

supplement: to add something else

symptoms: signs or evidence of an illness

techniques: specialized skills

Index

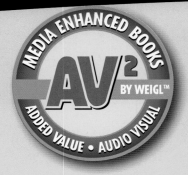

Log on to www.av2books.com

AV[2] by Weigl brings you media enhanced books that support active learning. Go to www.av2books.com, and enter the special code found on page 2 of this book. You will gain access to enriched and enhanced content that supplements and complements this book. Content includes video, audio, weblinks, quizzes, a slide show, and activities.

AV[2] Online Navigation

Book Pages
AV[2] pages directly correspond to pages in the book.

Audio
Listen to sections of the book read aloud.

Video
Watch informative video clips.

Key Words
Study vocabulary, and complete a matching word activity.

Embedded Weblinks
Gain additional information for research.

Quizzes
Test your knowledge.

Slide Show
View images and captions, and prepare a presentation.

Try This!
Complete activities and hands-on experiments.

AV[2] was built to bridge the gap between print and digital. We encourage you to tell us what you like and what you want to see in the future.

Sign up to be an AV[2] Ambassador at www.av2books.com/ambassador.